Living Beyond Expectancy

Also by Dr. Jerry L. Maynard, Sr

Maximize Your Potential
Building the Kingdom of God One Person at a Time
Leadership Pursuing Excellence

Also by True Vine Publishing Company

Charge the Walls
I Hear God in My Head
His Beauty for My Ashes
Seasons Come
Dare I Ask, What Am I Afraid Of?
Holy Ghost Explosion
Journeys in the Spirit
Words of my Mouth, Meditations of My Heart
On Butterfly Wings
Deliverance
Seeds of Greatness
Life… My Teacher
Positive Thinking Changed My Life
24 Minute Ministry Family Devotion
He that Finds a Wife
Who Are the Many
Night Before Dawn
The Other Woman
P.R.E.S.S.
From the Heart
My True Soul
When Boaz Comes

Living Beyond Expectancy

Bishop Jerry L. Maynard, Sr.

Nashville, TN

Living Beyond Expectancy
Dr. Jerry L. Maynard, Sr.
Copyright © 2008 by Dr. Jerry L. Maynard, Sr.
ISBN– 10 0-9786088-9-5
ISBN– 13 978-0-9786088-9-7

Published by
True Vine Publishing Company
P.O. Box 22448
Nashville, TN 37202

All right reserved. No part of this book may be reproduced in any form or by any electronic or mechanical means, including information storage and retrieval systems, without permission in writing from the publishing, except by a reviewer who may quote brief passages in a review.

Unless otherwise noted, all Scripture quotations are from the Holy Bible, King James Version.

Cover Design by Michael Thompson
www.MichaelDavidMedia.com

Printed in the United States of American—First Printing

To place orders for more books or get current information, contact us at www.CathedralPraise.org

For more information on the publisher, contact us at www.TrueVinePublishing.org

Table of Contents

A Balanced Life Through the Spirit 7

Carnal Living 11

Living in the Spirit 25

Spiritual Wisdom 31

Preparation 44

Position in Christ 68

Virtues of the Tongue 78

Releasing the Past 96

Right Now! 105

Christians Never Fail 111

Positive in Spite of Discouragement 124

Eternal Value 129

Conclusion: 138

Chapter 1
A Balanced Life Through the Spirit

Living beyond expectancy simply means living beyond that which you expect. The human mind is designed to expect only so much. In fact, it has been suggested that the conscious mind can only retain one dominant thought (either positive or negative) at a time. Your expectations are produced by the sum total of experiences you have had and the results that those experiences produced. Therefore, your human expectations can only take you so far. You expect that if you jump into a pool of water and do not know how to swim, you will sink and drown. You expect that if you leave your job, you will not have any money to pay bills. But God has a life that exceeds your natural expectations.

Now, as you learn to recognize this life that exceeds human expectations, you can't only focus your sights upward; you must include life here on earth. You should not fix your thoughts on that which is to come without giving some consideration to that which is. In other words, sometimes we are so interested in developing ourselves so that we can reach heaven that we miss a great deal of God's blessings here on earth.

In the African-American community, we as a people were so oppressed – physically, mentally, and spiritually – that we found our only hope in the "sweet by and by" or "in glory, where every day will be sweet Sunday." Many of us today still feel that the only time we will see better days is when we go to heaven. However, I want to declare that we are (and were) free to walk in God's blessings and to enjoy life here on earth before we reach heaven. And this freedom was not won by the noble efforts of Harriet Tubman, the Freedom Riders, Martin Luther King, Jr., Rosa Parks, or any other typical person. Jesus won it more than two thousand years ago. Yes, these valiant individuals fought relentlessly for freedom, but they were fighting for what was already theirs – for that which was won on Calvary.

The Lord wants us to have a balanced life; He does not want us to be so concerned about getting to heaven that we don't live good and fruitful lives here on earth. On the other hand, He does not want us to be so involved in earthly living that we forget that there is an eternal life. Sometimes we don't balance the two because we become too involved in one or the other. This is the root of the controversy over the so-called "prosperity message."

Many fail to realize that to preach about the material blessings of God is not to vitiate or denigrate spiritual blessings. The two are one in the same, for when you walk in spiritual blessings, material blessings follow. John said, "Beloved, I wish above all things that thou mayest prosper and be in health, even as thy soul prospereth" (3 John 1:2). Many have a problem understanding this because they don't understand the fullness of God.

Bishop Jerry L. Maynard

The Lord makes it possible for you to have a balanced life. This balanced life is important to living beyond expectancy. Many times, God blesses us, but the enemy quickly corrupts those blessings because we are not watchful and prayerful. God has blessed many people with the ability to set goals and objectives and perform very well, but these people become unbalanced. They put the blessings before God, or they become so engrossed in leaping to new heights that they forget about family and friends. Many times, they are so consumed by their success that they become stressed, acerbic people who cannot be used by God, thereby opening the door for the enemy to attack their bodies and ruin their testimony. Therefore, the first and most pertinent aspect of living beyond expectancy is to abandon...

Chapter 2
Carnal Living

In order to live beyond expectancy and enjoy a balanced life, you must ascend from carnality to spirituality; there is no other choice. Money and love are not the keys to a balanced life. Although this is the message the world perpetuates, it is completely misguided. In fact, all of the aspects of a godly, balanced life, if incorporated without God, still fail to produce a balanced life. Even if you have financial security, enjoy a steady relationship, and give to various charities, your life is yet unbalanced if you have not allowed God into your decision-making and all of your deeds, both good and bad, are carnally influenced.

The idea of carnal living has long been limited to a narrow range of a few sins that the church considers "lusts of the flesh." Carnal living in times past has been relegated to sex, alcoholism, drug abuse, card-playing, and watching and listening to secular movies and music. However, the Church of old failed to take a good look at the Word's definition of carnal living. First, you must understand that carnal living simply means living a life that submits to the carnal or fleshly desires and comforts.

Carnality can be found in all that we do, so it is impossible to avoid it. Tradition and ritualism in the Church is of a carnal nature. It has nothing to do with the Spirit; it helps people in a carnal way by providing a sense of stability or organization. The church bulletin is provided for our carnal comfort to help us understand where we are in order of service – although for some it's used to find out how much longer before one is free to go home and watch the game.

But the question begs to be answered: is the carnal aspect of life wrong? Is it wrong to need affection? Is it wrong to need order? Is it wrong to need laughter, to want the finer things of life, or to eat the delicacies of our culture? Is it wrong to have (hetero) sexual desires? The answer is an astounding NO! The carnality of man is not the sin that drives a wedge between God and humanity; it is man's overwhelming desire to put those carnal desires above God's desires that creates the chasm.

When Paul urged, "be not conformed to this world: but be ye transformed by the renewing of your mind" (Rom. 12:2), what he was warning against was being like the world, which holds the carnal needs in higher esteem than God. We are to be transformed, realizing that the Spirit must come first. You see, the world doesn't understand this concept. It's foolish to the worldly to give ten percent of one's income to a church and then believe God in regard to overdue bills. It's foolishness to them to fast (refrain from eating) all day. But when our minds are transformed and we walk in the Spirit, we can understand the power in these principles.

The Word lets us know that God is a Spirit: and they that worship him must worship him in spirit and in truth" (John 4:24). Living beyond expectancy has to be done in the spirit. Now, some may have a tough time understanding exactly what spirit living versus carnal living consists of. This is evident by the many souls who run the aisles of our churches only to return home to live in the same rut. What are they missing? They are missing a clear understanding of spiritual living. Once they can transcend carnal living, then they can transcend all carnal problems. As the Word clearly tells us, "Now the Lord is that Spirit: and where the Spirit of the Lord is, there is liberty" (2 Cor. 3:17).

Understanding the holistic nature of spiritual and carnal living is important to living beyond expectations. Carnal living is not just manifested in sex, drinking, and drugs. Carnal living is manifested in our refusal to obey God's voice when He tells us not to answer that midnight call from the companion who wants to come over. Carnal living is manifested in our refusal to call upon God to take away the pain that causes us to drink. In other words, carnal living cannot be summed up by the combination of alphabetical letters that make up the Ten Commandments. You might ask, what causes us to perform carnal deeds? And in so asking you will find the answer to carnal living.

According to Paul, carnal living is packaged in the following ideas: "Adultery, fornication, uncleanness, lasciviousness, idolatry, witchcraft, hatred, variance, emulations (jealousy), wrath, strife, seditions (divisions), heresies, envyings, murders, drunkenness, revellings, and such like" (Gal. 5:19-21).

Many will take a surface look at this scripture, avoid the connotations of these words, and consider themselves to be walking in the spirit, when in fact they are not. What do I mean? To go into detail would take another book, but I'll explain by using one example.

Idolatry: When we see this word, we imagine bowing down to a wooden calf or golden pig and worshipping it, praying to it, and sacrificing at its feet. So because we subscribe to Christian doctrine, we believe we are not carnally minded. However, we have cars, homes, companions, or other earthly possessions that we put before God. We have clothes that God tells us to give away, but we refuse to do so because they cost so much or because we just recently bought them. We have cars that we spend more money on than we're willing to give to the Church for Kingdom building. We have companions to whom we just can't say no because we're more afraid of losing them than we are in disappointing God.

This idolatry, in God's eyes, is as big a sin as sacrificing to a golden calf. Furthermore, 1 Samuel 15:23 explains that "stubbornness is as iniquity and idolatry." Yet many of us embrace our stubborn nature. We justify it by saying, "That's just who I am." We embrace it because we believe that it takes us further in life than being meek and gentle—which are the fruit of the Spirit. Little do we know that stubbornness is part of the fleshly or carnal work of idolatry. Paul explains that those who do such works "shall not inherit the kingdom of God" (Gal. 5:21).

No wonder God has postponed His coming for so long: many of us who think we are in right standing have a lot of corrections to make. The only way to overcome a carnal lifestyle is to know God's Word – not just the words in the Bible, but the Word of God. We must know the spirit of the words. The problem the Jewish religious leaders had in Jesus' day was that they knew the Law – the written words – but they didn't understand the spirit of the Law. Understanding the spirit of the Word will take us beyond the letters on the page and into the life within the words.

ESCAPING CARNALITY

There are many who are ensnared in a life of carnality and truly want to find freedom. I would be remiss to address and condemn carnal living without submitting the answer to escaping carnality. Now, many preachers would say, "Jesus will set you free," and though this is true to a degree, the fact is that escaping carnality is one of those deeds that we must perform ourselves.

There is one driving force behind a carnal lifestyle. Many are dealing with drinking, sex, lust, negativity, a foul mouth – whatever the case may be – and they don't know why these compulsions are so predominant in their lives and they can't shake them. The answer is very simple and consists of two factors: what we feed our spirits and with whom we associate.

As I mentioned, although many people wish to escape the carnal compulsions that lead them to sin, they don't make the concerted effort to micromanage their habits – case in point, sexual desires. Many people, particularly single people, struggle with their sexual urges. They don't understand why sex is on their minds on a daily basis or why they are constantly rebuking improper thoughts. They go through their days fighting images and thoughts and go home and carelessly turn on the television and watch it until they fall asleep.

So what, Preacher? What that person is overlooking is that the television displays thousands of sexual images and suggestions within the span of two or three sitcoms. We must realize that the old adage "You are what you eat" is not just a foolish statement our parents repeated; it is, in fact, a spiritual principle.

The spirit of a man never sleeps. It is always conscious and always feeding. If we go to sleep watching television, we are still receiving the sexual suggestions that flow from the television. When we drive our cars while listening to secular, sexually oriented music just because we like the beat, we don't realize that even though we don't know the words our spirit is picking up every idea presented in the song.

We wonder why we are so obsessed with sex, when in actuality, sex is all our spirits have been fed, and a spirit relies on what it is being fed. The first step to escaping carnality is continuously feeding our spirits things that are of the Spirit. We must reject everything that falls in line with the list of carnal attitudes presented in Galatians 5:19-21.

Bishop Jerry L. Maynard

Those of us who clean our homes on a regular basis have come to realize one unalterable irritation: no matter how much we dust, our furniture will have dust on it once again within 24 to 48 hours. Why is this? This happens because every time we take a step, sit down, open or shut the door, or turn on the air conditioner, there are particles being tossed into the air that must come back down. Likewise, our spirit is always collecting the dust of this world.

When we go to the grocery store, pass by the magazine rack, and see a half-naked woman, this is a dust particle falling on our spirit. When we are at the gym and the facility is playing a soundtrack of secular music, those songs are more dust particles. When we are on the bus, commuting to work, and we are forced to listen to the passenger sitting in the seat across the aisle curse out the person on the other end of his or her cell phone, this is carnal dust falling on our spirits. When we sin – by way of commission or omission – we collect more dust.

Living Beyond Expectancy

What happens if you don't wipe away all of that dust with the cleansing towels of prayer and biblical study? The dust builds up until it blocks the clear communication and spiritual interaction between you and God. That's right. Have you ever wiped your finger across a table that was very dusty only to realize that what you thought was mahogany was really red oak? The table was so dusty that you couldn't even tell its true color. This is what happens in the spirit. Our souls can get so dusty that we begin to lose our perception of what God is and isn't doing.

To counter this, we must continually dust our spirits. Looking at it from this perspective makes it clear why Isaiah suggests that our righteousness is as filthy rags (Isa. 64:6), for only by way of repentance, prayer, and study do we walk in righteousness through Jesus Christ. We must listen to tapes of our preachers' sermons or listen to recordings of the Bible. We must spend as little time watching television as possible unless we are watching something that will build our spirit man. I know men love sports, and there's nothing wrong with watching sporting events – but if watching them exposes you to pornographic suggestions, then you must align your priorities. There comes a time when we must accept the challenge presented by Jesus when He said, "If any man will come after me, let him deny himself, and take up his cross, and follow me" (Matt. 16.24).

Jesus was saying that there comes a time when you have to forsake those little pleasures for the greater cause. Jesus told the disciples that if their eyes offended them (caused them to sin), they should pluck them out (Matt. 5:29). We must resolve to cut off worldly desires because as long as we feed ourselves the ideologies and standards of this world, we will act on those influences.

Additionally, we must prudently judge those with whom we spend our time. First Corinthians 15:33 warns us, "Be not deceived: evil communications corrupt good manners." If we are to overcome our carnal nature, we must associate with people who are of like mind. When we are trying to fight the temptation to smoke, hanging around our old smoking partners at break time will not help. We cannot convert them when we are barely hanging on to our own convictions. We must separate ourselves from those who are not in one accord with us.

Amos 3:3 asks, "Can two walk together, except they be agreed?" This verse is very fitting in regard to associates and friends. Friends are a powerful influence in the life of any person because they help to shape us. Proverbs 27:17 explains that as "iron sharpeneth iron; so a man sharpeneth the countenance of his friend." Whether we want to admit it or not, we are influenced by our friends.

A bad friend is the worst kind of enemy because he or she will cause you to destroy yourself. At least we know that our enemies are out to destroy us, so we do the exact opposite of whatever they suggest. But a bad friend believes that he or she has your best interests in mind when he or she leads you astray, for "every way of a man is right in his own eyes" (Prov. 21:2).

Overcoming carnality all comes down to walking away from all carnal influences and replacing them those of the Spirit. It's that easy. If you love to watch *Sex and the City*, start watching Christian television. Yes, it's difficult to give up fleshly pleasures; welcome to the Christian walk. We can never receive our crown until we experience our cross. Peter explained it this way: "he that hath suffered in the flesh hath ceased from sin" (1 Pet. 4:1). In other words, when you learn to sacrifice the desires of the flesh for the cause of Christ, you will transcend the sinful nature. We must understand that suffering is not limited to physical pain; sometimes suffering consists of denying the flesh of some carnal pleasures.

Once we have escaped the bonds of carnality, we can begin our journey toward…

Chapter 3
Living in the Spirit

In 1 Corinthians 2:4 Paul explains that his speech is not that of "enticing words of man's wisdom, but in demonstration of the Spirit and of power." In this particular verse, the word "Spirit" is capitalized, indicating that Paul is referring to the Spirit of God and not the spirit of man. The Spirit of God gives you power. It is impossible to have the Spirit of God and not have power. It is impossible to have the Spirit of God and not have the anointing. When you walk in the Spirit, you have the power of God to do things just as God does them.

There is not a Spirit within God Himself and another spirit that He measures out to humanity. The Spirit you have is the same Spirit God has – the Spirit "that raised up Christ from the dead shall also quicken your mortal bodies" (Rom. 8:11). He will make you who you are supposed to be. Sometimes we don't understand where we are and what we have because of our own limited expectations. We simply expect God to come into us and make us feel good. However, the purpose of the anointing of God within us is not to make us feel good. The purpose of the anointing is to cause us to be like Him. Now, the point I'm about to make has proven to be controversial because many have not heard it before, and so they don't accept what I say. But that's fine; I'm going to say it anyway.

When the anointing of God comes upon you and you accept the tendencies of God, you accept the teachings of God, you accept the Word of God, the Word of God becomes a part of you, and you become part of Him, you don't become God, but you do become little gods – with a lower case "g."

God comes into you so that you may be energized as He is energized; that you may have wisdom as He has wisdom; and that the anointing of God may flow in your spirit as the anointing of God desires to flow.

Living Beyond Expectancy

This, as the disciples once said to Jesus, is a "hard saying" (John 6:60). So I'll explain it like this: What makes my children "Maynards"? It is the fact that my reproductive cells carry everything about me; everything I am is carried in these microscopic cells. One of these cells joined with an egg and the two united to bring forth a life. That life came from me.

The life that is created as a result is a product of me. If I am a Maynard, the life that comes from me has to be a Maynard. Others may call my children anything they please, but my children will always be Maynards.

God is spirit, and when the Spirit of God comes into you, you are not a devil or anything else. People may call you a whole lot of things, but you are a little god with a lower case "g." If God comes into you and He becomes the predominant Spirit and force in your life, you become a little god. So when the devil sees me, I let him know, "You are looking at my flesh, but that's not all of me. The real me that you should be disturbed about is not the fleshly me but the real me – the 'god' me who lives on the inside, the 'god' me who is the power and the force with which you have to reckon. You need to concern yourself about him, not Jerry Maynard, the fleshly person but Jerry Maynard the little god. Because when you mess with me, you are messing with a son of God."

Many people may not like this, but the Bible tells us that we are heirs of God. If we are heirs of God and joint heirs with Jesus Christ, how can we be less than sons? If the Spirit in you is not the same Spirit that was in Jesus Christ, you can't be a joint heir. The power that you have cannot be fathomed by the flesh, only by the Spirit. Imagine realizing and fully trusting in a power that exceeds the very apex of human possibility. Imagine walking in the strength – the very same strength – that created the heavens and earth. Imagine having the creative and constructive power in your tongue to speak to mountains and force them to move.

Living Beyond Expectancy

Is this not the epitome of living beyond expectation? Who would have expected Joseph, after being a slave and a prisoner, to become second in command of the greatest empire of the time in the matter of one day – with no elections, no revolution, just a two-second decision. Who would have expected Moses, a stuttering, pampered boy who enjoyed the luxury of the Pharaoh's royal court while his Jewish brothers slaved in the fields, to deliver the entire nation from Egypt? Who would have expected ruddy little David, the pretty boy who played the harp and wrote poetry, to become the greatest warrior and king this world has ever known? Who would have expected eleven cowardly disciples to turn this world upside down with the Gospel?

With the carnal mind, no one could have imagined these historical individuals and moments, but in the Spirit, all things are possible. We can live beyond expectancy because the expectations of God exceed what our mortal minds can conceive. In order to understand God's expectations, however, we will need…

Chapter 4
Spiritual Wisdom

Spiritual wisdom is that which exceeds the wisdom of even the wisest men. This wisdom looks into both the earthly and ethereal and understands the principles of both the natural and spirit. This is a wisdom that can see and understand the actions and motives of man. It is the wisdom that King Solomon obtained when He prays, "Give therefore thy servant an understanding heart to judge thy people" (1 Kings 3:9)

This wisdom, imparted only by the Spirit of God, sets you apart from mere men. This wisdom allows you to discern a person's heart and to see trouble before it even arrives. As Solomon writes, "A prudent man foreseeth the evil, and hideth himself" (Prov. 22:3, KJV) and "A wise man feareth, and departeth from evil" (Prov. 14:16). This kind of wisdom, as Solomon explains, is that principal thing that brings about a life beyond expectancy.

Spiritual wisdom is key to living beyond expectancy. In order to understand the importance of spiritual wisdom, you must first ask yourself what is wisdom. Wisdom is described in depth in Proverbs, which is best known as the "Book of Wisdom." In Proverbs, wisdom is described as a woman who cries out. We see that "length of days is in her (Wisdom's) right hand; and in her left hand riches and honour" (Prov. 3:16).

But what is wisdom beyond the abstract, metaphorical description and on a more practical, applicable platform? Is wisdom one's ability to read seventy books per year? Is wisdom revealed through the indefatigable exploitation of a voluminous vocabulary (in other words, the tireless use of one's rich vocabulary)? Is wisdom the ability to control and manipulate one's environment to one's own pleasure? Again I ask, what is wisdom?

WISDOM IS THE FEAR OF GOD

According to Proverbs 1:7, "The fear of the Lord is the beginning of knowledge." Our ability to philosophize, use elaborate words, calculate mathematical equations, or manipulate business projects has no bearing on wisdom. Wisdom is not intellect. Wisdom is not street smarts. Wisdom is not erudition. Wisdom is the divine impartation of understanding and knowledge for the purpose of succeeding in both carnal and spiritual dimensions.

Wisdom is given only through the mouth of God, for Proverbs 2:6 explains, "The Lord giveth wisdom: out of his mouth cometh knowledge and understanding." James instructs, "If any of you lack wisdom, let him ask of God" (James 1:5). James does not charge his readers to improve their reading skills, go back to college, or sit at the feet of the greatest philosophers of the age. He tells them to ask for wisdom from God and then mentions that God gives it freely. Wisdom is not hard to obtain.

Wisdom can only be found in fear – reverence – of the Lord. Only then is one truly walking in wisdom. So what is the fear of the Lord? According to Proverbs 8:13,

"The fear of the Lord is to hate evil: pride, and arrogancy, and the evil way, and the froward mouth." There are those who seek to walk in the wisdom of God but have not come to fear God yet, for they have yet to "hate" the "evil way." You may ask, "What does this mean? How can you say I don't fear God? I go to church every Sunday; I shout and run around the sanctuary. And I go to early-morning prayer." While these activities are good, I suggest you take a good look at David's approach to fearing God. Let's see what He "hated," as noted in Psalm 101: 1-5:

I will sing of mercy and judgment: unto thee, O Lord, will I sing. I will behave myself wisely in a perfect way. O when wilt thou come unto me? I will walk within my house with a perfect heart. I will set no wicked thing before mine eyes: I hate the work of them that turn aside; it shall not cleave to me. A forward heart shall depart from me: I will not know a wicked person. Whoso privily slandereth his neighbour, him will I cut off: him that hath an high look and a proud heart will not I suffer.

Living Beyond Expectancy

Now that you have read this scripture, I ask again: Have you really learned to hate the evil way? Well, let's explain hate. Hate is defined as feeling animosity or enmity toward; to detest; to feel great dislike or distaste for. In this scripture, David declares that he hates – he has animosity toward, detests, dislikes, and has distaste for – the works of those who turn aside (not the people themselves). He declares that he will set no wicked thing before his eyes.

How many of us discriminatingly choose the movies we watch? Now don't get me wrong. I am not one to preach that watching movies is a sin, but in the fear of God, you will not allow certain movies to be set before your eyes. People see movies in various ways. What offends some may not offend others. Some are extremely sensitive to foul language while others are so used to it they don't even notice when a foul word is spoken. How can we tell what needs to be censored?

Once again, we will refer to Galatians 5:19: "Now the works of the flesh are manifest, which are these; Adultery, fornication, uncleanness, lasciviousness, idolatry, witchcraft, hatred, variance, emulations (jealousy), wrath, strife, seditions (divisions), heresies, envyings, murders, drunkenness, revellings, and such like." Any movie that contains these ideas or is centered on these ideas is something that you should hate. It is something you should stay away from. Do you hate movies that glorify premarital sex, violence, hatred, adultery, murder, and gossip? Many of us do not hate such movies; in fact, we go around proselytizing and converting others on their behalf? Do your conversations with others consist of "Oh, girl, did you see *The Grudge?*" or "Have you seen *Ocean's Eleven?* You've got to see it." We don't realize we have just testified to the greatness of a worldly, ungodly influence even as we walk by soul after soul without even mentioning Jesus. If you were God, would you feel feared or revered?

David went on to mention "a froward heart" as well as one who slanders his neighbor privately. How many of us tolerate and even encourage gossipers? We should hate these works (the sins, not the people) and either confront a perpetrator in love or stay away from him or her altogether.

WISDOM KEEPS US ON THE RIGHT PATH

God gives us wisdom in order to "understand righteousness, and judgment, and equity; yea, every good path" (Prov. 2:9). Many have commented on the absolute necessity of initial failure in the life of a successful person. They suggest that all successful people meet success only after a great many failures. In fact, our greatest president, Abraham Lincoln, is quoted as saying, "Success is going from failure to failure without losing your enthusiasm."

Although setbacks are needed to strengthen us, we bring some setbacks upon ourselves because of a lack of wisdom. Wisdom is what keeps us from making mistakes to the detriment of our purpose. Mistakes are not always bad, but some can be detrimental.

No, I am not saying that your mistakes can stop God's will, for we know that God's Word will not return to Him void (Isa. 55:11). You must understand that God is infinite. If you need a lifetime to learn a lesson, He can wait. If He has to keep you alive for one million years, He has the power to do it.

Many times, your mistakes do just that: they cause your blessings to be delayed and, in some cases, suspended. Let's take Adam and Eve for example. They were not supposed to be evicted from the Garden. It was not intended for humanity to lose its eternal, spiritual connection to the Father. God's purpose for Adam and Eve was to enjoy the Garden for all eternity. They were to eat of all the fruit, including that of the Tree of Life. Adam and Eve could have enjoyed the Tree of Life in its fullness and lived forever, but they ate of the forbidden fruit from the Tree of the Knowledge of Good and Evil.

Living Beyond Expectancy

Due to a lack of wisdom – fear of God and hatred of evil – they produced a chain of events that has suspended the true purpose of God's creation and consequently has caused a world of havoc and sorrow for generations. When you don't walk in wisdom, you make mistakes that delay God's will for your life. The children of Israel were supposed to cross the Red Sea and go straight to the Promised Land. The trip was to take only three days on foot, but when the time came to take the land, the Israelites lost all wisdom and began doubting. Because of their doubt, a three-day trip became a 40-year suspension, and an entire generation missed out on God's blessings.

And lastly, Moses was initially supposed to escort the children of Israel into the Promised Land. But when the people aroused Moses' temper, which was evidently a sight to behold, Moses struck the stone to produce water instead of speaking to it as God had instructed him. Because of his actions, Moses was denied the opportunity to walk into the Promised Land. He was only allowed to observe it with his eyes. The writers of the Bible even found it noteworthy that Moses' eyes were "not dim" (Deut. 34:7). In other words, Moses was not too old; he wasn't even close to dying. He still had life in him. The only reason he died was because of his momentary lapse of wisdom. The Lord gives us His wisdom to direct us and keep us from falling off track.

SEEING BEYOND THE MOMENT

Spiritual wisdom also allows us to see beyond the moment. God gives us wisdom so that we can know not only who we are but also where we are going and what our purpose is. When we think of Jesus going to the cross, we consider it a shameful, terrible thing for the Jews to have crucified Him. But Jesus saw beyond their level of expectancy; He saw beyond what they saw. They saw pain, embarrassment, suffering, and death, and they thought they had defeated Him. But Jesus saw life beyond the cross, not just for Himself but also for you and me.

Living Beyond Expectancy

When you are going through trials and tribulations, don't look at your immediate blessings or downfalls. Look beyond your visible problems. Don't say, "I'm going through so that I'm a good Christian"; don't say, "I'm going through to show my faithfulness"; don't say, "I'm going through because I want God to pat me on the back"; instead, say, "Since God has chosen me to be an example, I'm going through this; but beyond my experience I see a great day; beyond my experience, I see a great future – and I see myself in the future, and I look much better than I do right now." There's a brighter day ahead!

You must realize that your expectations are limited to what you have been taught. You have been told that you are to expect "x" things at "x" times during your life, but these are finite ideas that man himself has given to you. These are expectations of results that will perish with your last breath. But, as we'll discuss in detail later, God is interested in bringing eternal results out of your life – results that surpass the most lofty imaginations of men.

Because of human limitations, some cannot fathom such a dimension, but in the sphere of God and life of God and wisdom of God, there are things that He has planned for us here on earth that we could never have imagined. As Paul said, "Eye hath not seen, nor ear heard, neither have entered into the heart of man, the things which God hath prepared for them that love him" (1 Cor. 2:9).

You have the capacity to think of life and death, and beyond that capacity you cannot comprehend. Yes, those of us who are saved know there is an afterlife; but even those of us who have been saved all of our lives and have experienced God in powerful ways cannot imagine the glory and splendor that God has in store for us. Yet God is not limited, and His capacity is far beyond our capacity. As a matter of fact, the Bible teaches us that His thoughts and ways are as a high above ours "as the heavens are higher than the earth" (Isa. 55:9). Therefore, whatever you think while here on earth is surpassed by something else that God has brought to the fore in the spirit realm, and He is waiting for you to gravitate to that wisdom that is found only in the Spirit so that His plans may be manifested for you in this earthly life.

After you have learned to fear God and walk in wisdom, then comes...

Chapter 5
Preparation

Jesus Christ, the only begotten Son of Almighty God, was sent to earth for a specific task. This task was to take only three years. Yet for some reason, the Father saw fit to have His Son come to earth in the form of a baby and wait around for 30 years. Why was this? The reason is because during those 30 years, Jesus was being prepared.

The next stage of living beyond expectancy is probably the most avoided area in Christendom. For some unknown reason, the people of God think that God's calling exempts them from training, although it is clearly stated throughout the Bible that the men of God went through periods of training and preparation. Proverbs 1:5 informs us that "a wise man will hear, and will increase learning," but, as the latter part of verse 22 reads, "fools hate knowledge."

Living Beyond Expectancy

There are many who have dreams that are not being realized because they fail to grasp the importance of proper preparation. They have dreams to be successful on their jobs or in their chosen field of expertise, or they dream of becoming powerful vessels of God, but they've become entangled in the web of immediate gratification. Proverbs 13:4 illustrates people like this by explaining that "the soul of the sluggard desireth, and hath nothing."

This verse describes "sluggards," who wait for opportunities to open to them instead of making opportunities. They make excuses as to why they cannot perform. They want things quickly. This scripture tells us that these individuals "desire" – they want a great many things. They may even consider their desires to be ambitions, but the fact is that they have nothing because they are not willing to work for anything. They are not willing to prepare themselves, train, and discipline themselves to obtain their dreams.

Consider Samuel, the prophet who anointed the first king of Israel, Saul, as well as the greatest king of Israel, David. Samuel's mother, Hannah, was barren, so she prayed to God for a child. And in return for the blessing of bearing a child, she promised to "give him [Samuel] unto the Lord all the days of his life" (1 Sam. 1:11). What did this mean? This meant the child would be sent to the Temple, where he would be trained and prepared to be a servant of God.

For some reason, the erroneous belief has been perpetuated that the anointing exempts individuals from training and schooling. But this is simply not true. Am I saying that only the educated are called of God? No, not at all. Neither am I suggesting that one cannot be used of God without a college degree. But I am saying that one cannot serve God effectively without being properly trained and prepared in some form. From Samuel to Jesus, training and preparation has been a vital part of a prosperous and productive life. Just as you take proper training for your earthly job seriously, so should you be serious about proper training for your Kingdom business.

PROPER VOCATIONAL TRAINING

The most wonderful thing about the God we serve is that He is a personal God. He is not a narcissist, cosmic Being who is concerned only about rules and praise. The God we serve is just as concerned about the little things in our lives as we are. The Word tells us that "the very hairs of [our] head are all numbered" (Matt. 10:30). A God who is concerned about the number of hairs on our heads – hairs that we indiscriminately cut away – must be concerned about our daily lives.

Many people long to have a friend to talk to about everyday problems, and don't realize that God is that Friend. No, God won't sit and listen to you complain and then tell you that you are so right and that others "shouldn't be acting like that." He won't tell you how you are totally correct in being upset and hurt because of your problems. Many of us want a friend who will nourish our complaints, but God will not do this. God will listen and then give you an answer or better understanding so that you can better deal with your issues. He is concerned about your spiritual life, and He is concerned about your earthly life. He wants you to do well in your chosen profession and the things to which you put your hands just as much as you do. In Deuteronomy 28:8 He declares He wants to "command the blessings upon... all that thou settest thine hand unto"; so, when you consider your occupation or vocation, you must understand that God wants you to be properly prepared.

Suppose one wants to design programs for computers. This person decides that instead of preparing through years of college training, he or she will go to church on Sunday and shout, scream, and dance around the church for that new career. Is it really possible that this person will leave the church that night, go home, and design a computer program? He or she will more likely be sucked into space by the gravitational pull of a giant comet than see this come to pass.

We need to understand one thing: yes, God can do all things, and there is nothing too difficult for Him, but there are some things He will not do! God will not do for you what you can do for yourself. God does what you cannot do. The reason He will not do what you are able to do is because you would not grow if He did. If parents held a newborn every day and never allowed that child to use its muscles or fend for itself in any way, that baby would soon experience muscular atrophy. That child's limbs would deteriorate into nothing, and eventually that baby could die.

Likewise, there are many progressive steps that you are required to take in order to grow and learn. These steps make you a stronger and better prepared individual for the challenges and ultimate victories that lie ahead. If God performed all the deeds that you could do on your own, whether physical, mental, or spiritual, you, too, would eventually die. God does not exempt you from preparing yourself for His calling.

Someone is thinking, "Yeah, but God told me I was going to open my own business, and my preacher teaches me that if God has anointed me to do a thing, He has already equipped me with everything I need to perform it." This is true. God has already placed within you the ability to attend your daily classes and do very well. God has already arranged for tuition for school; He has already set up internships for experience and has ordained the very location of your business. Indeed, He has put within you everything you need to prepare for and carry out your calling. But guess what: if you choose to avoid proper preparations, your business will not succeed.

We must realize that God reveals the end result of His calling, not the "in-between." When God says you are going to be a wealthy and prosperous businessperson or an anointed preacher who will travel the world, He is indicating the end result of what He has called you to be.

There is an in-between that you must travel through to get to the end. Many people make the mistake of quitting their jobs and leaving stable positions because they receive God's word for their lives; instead of getting ready for the time of preparation, they decide to jump right into the fullness of their calling.

KINGDOM SIGNIFICANCE

But really, why would God – who is spirit, whose focus is on the reconciliation of souls, and whose business is soul business – be concerned about my business? Good question. Because you are an ambassador of Christ, every aspect of your life has a heavenly effect. Every task is a Kingdom-ordained assignment. You don't get jobs just so you can pay bills. The Bible tells us that "God shall supply all your need according to his riches in glory" (Phil. 4:19). So why are you working? Deuteronomy 8:18 suggests that God "giveth thee power to get wealth, that he may establish his covenant." It doesn't state that He gives you power to get wealth so that you can provide for your own needs. You are blessed with finances not primarily to pay bills but to establish God's kingdom. The most important part of your paycheck is the portion that goes into the Kingdom – into helping God's people and supporting ministries – for it is that part that ensures the continuous flow of the rest.

Money you pay to the gas and electric companies, car notes, and credit cards is not what will return to you a blessing that you won't have "room enough to receive" (Mal. 3:10). Car payments don't keep the Good News spreading across the world. You must see your job as providing you with a way to further the Kingdom, not as a way to pay bills. Jesus showed us that we don't need to worry about bills when He sent Peter to retrieve his taxes from a fish's mouth. When you are walking in God's will, He will provide your every need.

Now, let's not confuse what I'm saying. I'm not suggesting that you give your whole paycheck to the church and trust God to pay your bills – unless God tells you to do so. The ability to pay your bills is a byproduct of being a good steward of the money God has given you. But when you put bills before Kingdom business, you've lost your understanding of the purpose of your job. With such a mindset, people reject the instructions of God for fear of losing material goods.

When I talk about putting Kingdom business above earthly business, I am speaking from experience. As a young man working for the government of Indiana, I was making six figures, living in the nicest neighborhood, driving the best of cars. Life was wonderful for this young man who had come from nothing. But then God called me to full-time ministry. He told me, "I've called you to pastor." When He told me to leave my job, I considered my bills, that nice paycheck, and the fact that I had a wife, and I did not agree with God's plan. I believed that my job provided the beautiful life I was living – a life that I felt full-time ministry couldn't offer.

I learned the hard way that it's better to obey and trust God when He tells us to step out into thin air on the wings of faith than to hold on to the guardrails of carnal security. For those guardrails can be broken down by a simple change of opinion. What God knew that I didn't know was that a new administration was about to be put into place and that the new governor was not too fond of the work I was doing in the area of civil rights and securing racial equality in the state and country.

What God knew that I didn't know was that this governor was going to do all he could to ruin my reputation and the progress I had made. Had I believed, trusted, and walked in God's promise to provide all my needs, I would not have had to go through the stress that the new administration put me through. Yet I was free through it all, in spite of the governor's attempts to prosecute me and slander my character. I passed right through the governor's attack just like Jesus passed through the crowd of people who wanted to throw Him off a cliff "headlong" after He publicly announced Himself as the Anointed One.

Your vocation has Kingdom significance. It is just as important a tool for God's use as is the holy lectern. It fits in with God's plan for His people to be in charge. This is why Paul commanded the Colossians, "Whatsoever ye do, do it heartily, as to the Lord, and not unto men" (3:23). When you work unto God and not for the approval of man, God will make sure you are promoted because "when the righteous are in authority, the people rejoice: but when the wicked beareth rule, the people mourn" (Prov. 29:2). I'll reiterate the old cliché: your life is the only Bible some people will ever read. In all things, you must demonstrate excellence; you must shine in the darkness in all ways because your influence will draw souls.

PREPARATION FOR SPIRITUAL MINISTRY

You must prepare for spiritual ministry. If you are going to advance beyond the norm, you cannot be slack concerning the Word. You must thirst for understanding of God and His will for your life. As Paul instructed Timothy, "Study to shew thyself approved unto God, a workman that needeth not to be ashamed, rightly dividing the word of truth" (2 Tim. 2:15). In today's difficult theological atmosphere, we cannot afford to assume that by simply knowing the Ten Commandments and the books of the Bible, we will win souls to Christ.

We must plant the Word in our spirits, first of all for our own growth and secondly so that we may sow it into the lives of others. We must seek God daily, pray continuously, fast, and consecrate ourselves so that we may be vessels ready for use. How would you feel if you were thirsty for water and looked in your cabinet only to realize that all the glasses and cups were dirty and in the dishwasher waiting to be washed? Wouldn't that be a very frustrating feeling? There you'd be, needing a clean vessel but unable to find one.

We are like those dirty dishes when we refuse to prepare ourselves for spiritual ministry. Preparation must involve not only training and schooling but also spiritual cleansing and consecration. We must set ourselves apart from the world. This is what Paul was saying in Romans 12:1 when he wrote, "Present your bodies a living sacrifice."

When the Israelites presented an animal sacrifice to God, it had to be dressed and presented in a specific fashion. One could not just offer a dirty or blemished sheep that just so happened to be straggling at the back of the herd. The sacrifice had to be acceptable to God. Likewise, we cannot present ourselves while we are in just any condition spiritually.

When we go to church to worship God, we must not enter in just any spiritual manner. If we have an attitude, or if we're frustrated because of the traffic on the way to church, we need to release our negative feelings. If we have been arguing with or nagging our spouse, we need to set things right before we present ourselves to God. Jesus dealt with this matter specifically when He said, "If thou bring thy gift to the altar, and there rememberest that thy brother hath ought against thee; Leave there thy gift before the altar, and go thy way; first be reconciled to thy brother, and then come and offer thy gift" (Matt. 5:23-24). Jesus was saying that our spirits and our service must be presented in purity. We must be spiritually prepared to worship, and we must be spiritually prepared to serve. God is looking for clean vessels who will serve those lost souls who desire to join Him at His table.

Imagine you are a businessperson and you have an important client coming to your home for dinner. You know this night could make or break the deal. When the potential client arrives, you put your best foot forward because you know that everything he/she sees will reflect on you and the sort of person you are. Everything goes well for a while; the client is enjoying the conversation, and he/she's interested in what you have to offer. But then your cook brings in the main course – on filthy plates. The glasses have spots and there are food particles on the dishes.

This spectacle reflects terribly on you and the type of service you provide. You can't even keep your own dishes clean; how can you be trusted to handle the affairs of this client's business? Isn't this what we do in our Christian walk? We attract people with our tirade of "Praise God, I'm blessed and highly favored" talk; our conversation draws them in, and they are interested in hearing something about this Jesus we claim to serve, but when it is time to serve the main dish, our dirty, unprepared spirits begin to reveal themselves. Others watch us get raging angry in traffic and start waving that special finger. They see us snap at work and use words that aren't found in the Bible. Then, they say to themselves, "If this kind of dirt is in the house of God, how can I improve my plight?" It is imperative for our own sakes as well as the lost that we prepare ourselves for God's service. It must be a daily cleansing, for we never know when our service will be needed.

Prepared "In Season, Out of Season"

Statistics show that the Muslim religion is the fastest growing religion in America today, while Christianity is declining the fastest. Why? What is it that draws people toward idolatry and away from Christianity? The answer is simple: saints who are not properly prepared, as Paul stated, to "be instant in season, [and] out of season" (2 Tim. 4:2). In other words, because of our lack of preparation through studying, interacting, and serving, the Body of Christ is losing its ability to reach people where they hurt and to minister in any and every situation.

We must be prepared to give a word of life to any individual, in any situation, at any time. We understand that this wisdom does not come from us but from God, and that we must have the Word planted in our hearts so that God can bring it out of us. According to Jesus, the Holy Spirit "shall teach [us] all things, and bring all things to [our] remembrance, whatsoever [God has] said unto [us]" (John 14:26). There is responsibility implied within this verse – the responsibility to read and to hear the Word of God.

How can the Holy Spirit teach us if we don't go to class? As children, we had to go to school. The school was there and the teachers were there, but if we didn't go, we couldn't be taught. Likewise, if we don't seek God's face, He can't tell us anything. Recall from the previous section that there are some things God will not do. We must understand that God will *not* make us read the Bible. Only when we read the Bible can the Holy Spirit bring to our remembrance the things Jesus has told us.

This is encouraging, for it lets us know that God does not require us to walk around with a grand encyclopedia of principles and revelations; He does not require us to know the Bible verbatim. All He wants us to do is allow Him to plant the seed of the Word in our spirits so that He may draw it out in due season. There are hurting people in the world and the wisdom and revelatory words God places in us are not there so that we can sit back and think about how deep we are. Furthermore, they are not to be held until we can preach about them before a congregation.

EMOTIONALISM VS. PROPER PREPARATION

We have confused the anointing of God with whooping and squalling. We don't have to go to school or even have to study the Bible to whoop and squall. We assume that if we can get our church members excited enough with our fancy wordplay, gestures, puns, and verbal gimmicks, they won't recognize that we don't know the difference between the Beatitudes and a Bad Attitude. They won't realize that we're teaching people that King David built an ark that took the children of Israel over the Michael Jordan River while they were running from Goliath. If we say something false just right, they'll never know the difference.

Living Beyond Expectancy

I once attended a conference as a young preacher where the keynote speaker pulled me and a few other preachers aside in order to make a point. He told us that He could tell people anything at all as long as he whooped and hollered. He predicted they would enjoy every minute of his sermon without realizing or even caring about the truth or content of what he was saying. When the time came, the preacher began his tirade. He screamed at the people, telling them they were "low-down, dirty dogs." They were "no good and never going to be any good." All the while, the people grew more and more excited. Despite the fact that he was denigrating them, despite the fact that not a word he was saying was edifying or even had anything remotely to do with the Gospel, the people loved his discourse.

When we encourage our preachers for whooping and tell them that their sermons were powerful simply because they were emotional, we do a disservice to them, to ourselves, and to the thousands of other souls who will not be fed as a result of that preacher's delusional sense of effectiveness. A preacher's sermon should add substance to the lives of those who hear it. A preacher is to "heal the brokenhearted, to preach deliverance to the captives, and recovering of sight to the (spiritually) blind, [and] to set at liberty them that are bruised" (Luke 4:18). Otherwise, that preacher's message is vain, and there is no more time for vain babbling. It doesn't matter how many people fall out in the floor or run the halls or pews. Stage presence can never substitute for proper spiritual preparation.

THE THIRSTING SOUL CANNOT BE FOOLED

When we're talking one-on-one to a hungry soul, we can't disguise a lack of preparation. Either our mouths are flowing with "rivers of living water" or they are not (John 7:38). Although a crowd of emotional spectators may not notice that we're lacking, that single thirsty soul will know for sure. You can't tip an empty glass of water over a dehydrated man's face and expect him to be replenished.

Living Beyond Expectancy

Paul told the Corinthians that he "came not with excellency of speech" (1 Cor. 2:1). Likewise, if we want people to get involved in the things of God, we need to simply talk to them about Him without trying to influence their thinking with fancy verbiage. The Gospel should not be mysterious. It shouldn't be so deep that the average person cannot understand it. The reason theologians and preachers create a fog of theological, philosophical mumbo-jumbo is to maintain an air of superiority by keeping others in the dark.

The "picture" of salvation is already painted – you don't have to repaint or embellish it. God sent His Son, His Son gave His life, then died on the cross, rose from the dead, went back to the Father, and now acts as Mediator between man and God. Amen. However you try to paint it, that's the story.

Unfortunately, due to the slackness of many, the Body of Christ is offering a lot of empty glasses. On the other hand, the Muslims and those of other religions are reaching out and making impact. They are studying Christianity and forming their arguments against it; then they're taking those arguments to those dehydrated souls whom we have left on the side of the road with empty glasses. They are convincing those souls that their false religion is the water that will replenish them. In fact, these false religions take advantage of the empty glass that we have offered and fill it with dirty water. The vast majority of false religions, particularly Islam, take a great deal of their doctrine straight from the Bible and then add a few specks of dirty religiosity.

Thirsty men and women are drinking of the water that these false religions are offering because a dehydrated individuals will accept water whether it's clean or dirty. And they will appreciate and cling to the person who gave it to them. The world has prepared itself to reach out to people, and the Church must do the same.

Once you have prepared yourself to realize your dreams and live beyond expectancy, the enemy is sure to attack. Now begins the most exciting and challenging time of your journey. This road will be one that meanders, dips, and spikes, and to navigate your way through with confidence, you must understand your...

Chapter 6
Position In Christ

After you have prepared yourself for your future, prayed and communicated with God concerning your next step, and been told by God to step out and perform His will, you are going to have to know who you are in Christ. This is important because no matter how anointed you are, there will always be situations and people who will attempt to make you feel inferior and that you are less than who you really are. There will be times when you are overlooked, passed up, or – even more painful – utterly rejected.

There will be times when you do not have a dime in your pocket and you'll wonder how someone with a calling and anointing can be in such a state of despair. You will wonder if you are really called at all – if you're really as anointed as you think and if you're really positioned in God like you thought you were. It is during these times that you must know beyond the shadow of a doubt your position in Christ.

Let us consider Elijah, the prophet of God, who was able to call down fire from heaven and yet sat in desolation while being fed from the beaks of ravens. How many of us, after getting used to eating filet mignon and porterhouse steaks with dignitaries while sitting in seats of honor, would be happy having a scavenger bird bring us a doggy bag of the rotting lunch it just found? How many of us would question our position in the Body of Christ? We would begin wondering what we'd done wrong and why God was angry with us.

God wants you to get to the point where you know your royal position beyond the shadow of a doubt. Whether or not you have money, jewelry, or nice clothes, you must be secure in your position in God and walk in your authority. John the Baptist was a prime example. No question, he must have looked, as we say in today's vernacular, "a hot mess." His beard was shabby and crusted over with honey and cricket legs. His body reeked of mildewed camel fur. But none of this mattered to him. He was confident in his anointing and his position in the Kingdom. He understood that whether he wore camel fur or the most expensive robe, his clothes did not make him who he was. He was ordained and created before the foundation of the earth to be the "voice of one crying in the wilderness" (Matt. 3:3). Whether or not people could stand the stench that exuded from his body, he was secure in his position in the Kingdom. It didn't matter that he had to eat locusts while others were enjoying the fat of the lamb. It didn't matter that he had no property while others owned cattle aplenty.

When you know your place in Christ, you can transcend the temporal desires of this carnal realm, realizing that you can indeed have luxurious things, but they do not make you who you are. What makes you who you are is the position you have in the Kingdom. Once you realize this, you can walk the streets while possessing the same confidence you would have if you were riding in a Jaguar sports coupe. You can wear your one suit with the same confidence you'd have if you were wearing a tailor-made suit.

But here is the key to it all; here is the point we don't realize: when you know your position, you can be like Jesus, who didn't posses the wherewithal to get material things but could command it to exist. In other words, Jesus didn't have a six-figure income, but because He knew His position with the Father, He commanded the same respect and benefits as one with such a job. Jesus simply walked up to people and told them, for example, "Zacchaeus, make haste, and come down; for to day I must abide at thy house" (Luke 19:5).

Wow! Isn't this the kind of authority that only a man with infinite financial resources could command? Imagine your father was the king of the world, and you were the prince of the world. Would you ever need to approach a stranger and say, "Hey, I need a few dollars; can you give me what's in your pocket, please?" or "Listen, Mr. Banker, I need $200 thousand for a home and a 5% interest rate." Of course not – because whatever you required could be taken care of without the help of anyone else. In fact, were you to actually acquire someone's help, you would be doing him or her a favor, knowing that your father would reward that person for his or her generosity.

When you know your position in Christ – the fact that you are a coheir with Christ, giving you the same authority to command the resources of God as Christ did – you won't be so uptight when money is scarce. When you understand in your spirit that your heavenly Father is the King of the world, making you the prince or princess of the world, you will walk in confidence as Jesus did and command this kingdom to submit itself to you – the heir of the heavenly Kingdom.

You come from the greatest Kingdom; you can overpower the negative forces of your life and the lives of others with the Kingdom power you have. Jesus has al-

Living Beyond Expectancy

ready given you permission to perform every deed He performed here on earth. He has even said, "Greater works than these shall [you] do; because I go unto my Father (John 14:12). Therefore, you can speak to the elements of earth and say, "Peace, be still," and the elements must obey (Mark 4:39). You just need to know your position.

NO INFERIORITY IN CHRIST

When Paul ministered to the church of Corinth, he had a lot to contend with. The church of Corinth dealt with a great deal of doubt and fear. The Corinthians didn't know who they were in Christ. Many of them were Jewish and some were Gentiles, and the Jewish people felt superior to the Gentiles. The Gentiles often took a place that was subservient to the Jews. When you don't know who you are, you abide by one of two extremes: superiority or inferiority. The Jews adhered to the extreme of superiority, believing they were more than they truly were, while the Gentiles adopted an attitude of inferiority, believing they were less than they truly were. Because the Gentiles were not of Jewish descent, they were looked down upon. The only thing they had going for them was the fact that they believed in Jesus.

You must come to the realization that any time God asks you to do a work, it will lie beyond your capability. It will require you to step into an arena with which you are not familiar – and those who are already familiar with the arena will scrutinize, criticize, and discriminate against you. Yet this is part of God's plan. He does not wish to diminish you or pick on you. He does this to show forth His glory. He sends you into unfamiliar territory so that you will have to trust in Him every step of the way. According to Proverbs 6:16-17, God hates pride, which is a natural tendency of the human psyche. Whenever we as humans achieve a major feat, it is our nature to want to take full credit for it. However, there is a no-tolerance rule for pride when it comes to the vessels of God. So if we are going to be used of God, we must all face the discrimination and scrutiny of those who feel superior.

This human fight for superiority has existed forever. Racism is nothing new to the world. The Civil Rights movement of the 1950's through the 1960's constituted just one of many race explosions. In Africa, certain tribes have despised other tribes; in Europe, the upper classes discriminated against and were prejudice toward the poor; and Paul had to teach the Gentile Christians that their position was not about blood lineage or being amongst the original Disciples – it was about the Spirit of God, who takes us from the bottom of our experience to the peak of God's excellence.

In God's excellence, the Gentiles were able to stand just as tall as those who were Jewish by birth. Likewise, the Body of Christ today ought to consist of the most influential people on the planet because we have the most powerful Being, God Almighty, living in us. This is something to be excited about.

Some of us measure ourselves against others because of our background. Our parents might not have brought us up in the church; as a matter of fact, we may have led a terrible, sinful life. But we must understand that once God saves us, once God sanctifies us, once God gives us a place in the Body of Christ, we have just as much a right to stand before Him as a holy person as does anyone else. It doesn't make any difference how long we've been part of the Body. This truth was made evident when Jesus taught the parable about the workers in the vineyard. He told them He would pay "whatsoever [was] right" (Matt. 20:4). There were those who had agreed earlier in the day to work for what was amounted to approximately a penny. Early in the day, they agreed to work, and thus they labored all day. There were also those who arrived at the very end of the work experience and only worked one hour, and they received just as much as those who had worked all day.

What God is trying to show us through this example is that it doesn't make any difference when you come to Christ; the mere fact that you come and that you agree

Living Beyond Expectancy

to accept the stipulations He makes in relation to your being "employed" entitles you to the payment He offers all His workers. God allows us to come into His presence irrespective of who we are. He says to us, "It does not matter to Me where you've been, how long you've been there, or what you've done – the mere fact that you've come and said, 'Lord, have mercy on me, forgive me of my sins, blot out my transgressions, save my soul – and God, I thank You, not only because You are able to save me but because You have done it – and I receive it in Jesus' name,' is good enough for Me." Praise the Lord for our position in Him.

Now that we know our position and have been grounded and established in Him, we must be cautious not to tear ourselves down by understanding the…

Chapter 7
Virtues of the Tongue

This last principle of realizing your dreams truly cannot be overemphasized. Enough cannot be written about the importance of the use of our tongues.

The use of your tongue has extreme significance regarding your ultimate achievements. You could master all the aforementioned steps to realizing your dreams and living beyond expectancy, but unless you gain total control of your tongue, you would be headed for utter disaster. James explains to us that "if any man offend not in word, the same is a perfect man, and able also to bridle the whole body" (James 3:2). Many people spend thousands of dollars on psychiatric treatment and read tons of self-help books all in an effort to better themselves – to perfect themselves – but here, James explains that there is one key to perfection: controlling your tongue. If you can control your tongue, you can control your entire body.

Living Beyond Expectancy

This is a powerful concept, for it indicates that the tongue and the way it is used impacts both the way you think and the way you act. When you say, "I can't," you don't. When you say, "I can," you do. The tongue is the steering wheel in our vehicle to destiny. James further develops this idea when he compares our tongues to ships at sea: "Though they be so great, and are driven of fierce winds, yet are they turned about with a very small helm, whithersoever the governor listeth" (James 3:4). James marvels, as do I, at how such a small member can change the very course of our existence.

This principle concerning the power of the tongue is not merely a Christian concept. This principle is a universal law. Those who have invested in hearing motivational speakers and attending seminars know that one of the major points stressed by every speaker, whether Christian or non-Christian, is the importance of speaking positive things about oneself and about one's dreams. The world calls this "positive affirmations"; the Body of Christ calls it faith. The tongue is so potent that Solomon declares that it has the ability to determine "death and life" (Prov. 18:21). He assures us that "a man shall be satisfied with good by the fruit of his mouth" (12:14).

To understand the power of your tongue, you must first recognize where all your power comes from. In Genesis 2:7 we read that God "formed man of the dust of the ground, and breathed into his nostrils the breath of life; and man became a living soul." God breathed into man not just air (that is, oxygen) but His very Spirit. The breath of God was the Spirit of God.

Do you remember discussing the fact that when we have within us the Spirit of God, we become little gods? This same principle applies to God blowing His spirit into us and giving us life. The Person who said, "Let there be light" (Gen. 1:3) breathed the very essence of His being into man. Our life Source consists of the same power that created the heavens and earth just by speaking them into existence.

Living Beyond Expectancy

If your life source is the Spirit of God, you cannot help but have the same power that He, the Source, has. Because God could "speak" creative power, you can do the same. Because God said, "Let there be light," and light came out of darkness, you can speak light into the midst of your darkness. No, you cannot speak light into a dark room because God has already created the resource to provide that need. If a room is dark, go buy a light bulb. But you can speak light into your darkest situations. This chapter is going to show you just how to do just that.

A POWERFUL WEAPON

Why do we use such powerful weapons – our tongues – so carelessly? The government requires that persons who purchase a handgun attend a class to learn the proper usage of that weapon. The underlying, unspoken rule is that such a powerful instrument should not be wielded by anyone who is not trained to handle it. Such a weapon has too much life-altering potential to be handled haphazardly.

In Revelation, Jesus is described as having "a sharp sword, that with it he should smite the nations" coming out of His mouth (19:15). What was this weapon? It was the Word of God. Jesus will come with the Word and smite the nations. The power that Jesus will use to destroy His enemies is the power you possess. You have a choice: you can use your weapon for Kingdom-building and self-building, or you can use it for self-destruction.

You might wonder, "Why would I use it for self-destruction?" Why, indeed, would anyone knowingly use a powerful weapon against himself or herself for any reason other than suicide? Please catch the following point: speaking negatively about ourselves or our dreams is a form of suicide. If a statement is not going to push you forward, it does not need to be said – period. It's neither foolishness nor naïveté to absolutely refuse to make a negative declaration.

Understand that your tongue has the same potential to kill as does a gun. Although this sounds extreme, it is definitely a fact. A bullet has the power to harm and possibly kill the body, but the tongue has the power to harm and possibly kill the spirit, which has a more destructive effect than any fleshly death. Solomon asked the question, "A wounded spirit who can bear?" (Prov. 18:14). You must see your tongue as a weapon – one that you must be trained to use. You must discipline yourself to utilize this weapon to fight your way to victory, prosperity, life beyond expectancy, and – ultimately – realizing your dreams.

LEARNING TO USE YOUR TONGUE

We have discussed the acquisition of wisdom. To control your mouth, all you have to do is ask God for wisdom. What will God tell you? He won't give you a list of do's and don'ts. No, that's not what God will do. What He will do is tell you to hush up when you begin to speak carelessly. What He will do is tell you, "Don't say a word about the sin you caught brother John in today." What He will do is tell you, "Don't speak one negative word today." It will then be up to you to obey. It's that easy. Many times, we speak sickness on ourselves, we speak poverty on ourselves, we speak injury on ourselves, and we don't even know that we've done so.

Have you ever had a sniffle and a little tickle in your throat? What was the first thing you said? "Oh, no, I'm coming down with a cold." Have you ever wanted to eat out for lunch but looked into your wallet to find no money? What did you say? "I'm broke; I can't go out to eat." Have you ever told someone, "I'm so clumsy"? What were you doing when you said these things? You were empowering negative traits and influences.

Some people say, "Well, it (having a cold, lacking finances, etc.) is just a fact. Being a Christian doesn't make you blind." I submit to you that Christians must not pay attention to earthly facts but to God's Word. The earthly facts say we are sick; the Word says that "with his stripes we are healed" (Isa. 53:5). The earthly facts say we don't have money and the car is about to be repossessed.

The Word says that God provides for "all your need according to his riches in glory by Christ Jesus" (Phil. 4:19).

As foolish as it may seem to the flesh to speak in opposition to what you see, your victory and the realization of your dreams will only come as a result of doing this very thing. Even in the midst of your trouble, you must speak what you know God has promised. You must speak what you know He has ordained and continue to speak it until you see the desired outcome. Sometimes is takes a day, sometimes it takes years, but you must speak the Word of God and believe it above earthly appearances.

SAY WHAT YOU WANT

Recall that Jesus taught His disciples, "If ye have faith as a grain of mustard seed, ye shall say unto this mountain, Remove hence to yonder place; and it shall remove; and nothing shall be impossible unto you" (Matt. 17:20). What did Jesus tell the disciples to say to the mountain? He instructed them to tell the mountain the expected and desired action or result. This is how you are to approach issues you confront, whether challenges, problems, or ambitions. Yes, the fact is that there is a mountain in your way. Yes, the fact is that the mountain is big. Yes, the fact is that the mountain presents a problem. But Jesus didn't instruct the disciples to tell the mountain, "You are a big mountain. I'm going to have problems because of you, mountain. I can't afford to walk all the way around you, mountain." No, Jesus did not tell the disciples – or us – to speak words of acknowledgment. Rather, He told them – and us – to command the mountain.

Have you ever approached a very busy person? He or she will pick up his or her eyes from present task with a very recognizable look – one that relays a strong and clear message: "I don't have time for all the useless details…. WHAT DO YOU WANT?"

Likewise, when a problem presents itself, you are not to waste time by conversing with the problem; you are to command the problem. You don't have time to find out why a problem is so big or why it chose to attack you in particular. You need simply to address the problem: "Problem, move!" When you look in your wallet and see no money, don't talk about how nice it would be to have more money or about how you really need five dollars. Instead, say, "Money, I command you to increase." When you wake up with a tickle in your throat, say, "Sinuses, I command you to clear up in Jesus' name. By His stripes I am healed, so I command you to submit to the Word of God."

Sometimes the results are immediate. Other times, you'll have to wait a while and seek God's face for instruction. Sometimes the alleged problem is not the real issue; we are the issue. Sometimes even as we are yelling at a mountain to move out of our way, God taps us on the shoulder and says, "Are you finished screaming at that mountain? Good, because you're supposed to be going the opposite direction." Many of us have experienced this in regard to our finances and health. We scream at the devil to release us from the chains of debt, but moments after we get off of our knees, we go shopping and use our credit cards to pay for what we want. We finance furniture or cars. And all the while, Satan is saying, "I appreciate the acknowledgment, but you're doing a fine job without me." There are those of us who fight high blood pressure and other health issues while yelling at the devil to release our bodies. All the while, we continue to consume unhealthy foods. Sometimes we need to use our tongues to rebuke ourselves. We need to tell ourselves, "No, you cannot eat this" or "No, you cannot spend money on that."

SPEAKING YOUR DREAMS

Have you ever spoken about an idea but failed to put it to action? Maybe you told a friend that you had an idea about a self-draining pot. Perhaps you told others about this wonderful idea as well, but you never stepped out to make it a reality. The next thing you knew, while watching television, an infomercial came on, promoting a new self-draining pot. You scream, "That was my idea!"

Living Beyond Expectancy

What happened? You spoke an idea into existence and then left it for someone else to claim. When we speak a word, we are sowing seed. Jesus told a parable about seed falling on good ground, rocky ground, and thorny ground. Your words are spiritual seeds that fall into your spiritual field of destiny. Many of us pour seed after seed into the field, but because we don't understand or we don't truly believe the power of our words, we leave every field we sow unattended. This is why James writes that "a double minded man" should not think "he shall receive any thing of the Lord" (James 1:7-8). A double-minded man who is desultory in life, jumping from one idea to another, planting field after field of creative ideas but leaving them unattended, will not receive anything from God.

Have you ever tried to chase down a very hyperactive dog? The dog's agility and ability to change direction in a split second make it almost impossible to catch. After a period of running to and fro, trying to catch the dog, you eventually stop running. You stand in one place, having decided to let the dog expend its energy until it comes back home on its own.

This is how we act with God. We speak a mouthful of ideas. One day we want to be an entrepreneur, the next day we want to preach, then we want to sing, and then we want to do missionary work. The next week, we have an invention we want to patent. We speak all these things into existence but we abandon every field. Pretty soon, God stops and says, "I'm not moving another step."

When we leave our fields unattended the time for harvest eventually arrives, and someone else walks onto a field of prosperity that we planted, clears out the few weeds that have accumulated, cleans it up, and claims the bounty. That's why we discover that our ideas are making money for other people. We have got to come to the understanding that when we speak a word, that word is manifested when it leaves our mouth. It may not become manifest in a visible or tangible way for a while, but once we speak the word, we begin a process of birth.

THE IMPORTANCE OF POSITIVE SPEECH

You must speak positive, life-producing words at all times. Byrd Baggett, author of *The Book of Excellence: 236 Habits of Effective Salespeople*, writes, "Don't waste your energy on negative gossip." This principle illuminates an aspect of speaking to which many people do not pay attention. Speaking expends energy, and anyone who has spoken to a very negative person realizes that negative speech drains energy.

Though it's impossible to explain the process, simply sitting and listening to a negative person – while not utilizing any energy at all – will leave you drained of all energy once the person leaves. You'll find you need to take a breath of fresh air. If simply listening to negativity is draining, how much more does speaking negatively drain a person? When you speak negatively, you suck the life out of your ideas and ambitions.

As every negative word you speak comes out of your mouth, it takes with it a bit of your optimism and hope. In essence, your excitement and ambition has to kick into overdrive to compensate for your negative talking. Many of us are so accustomed to speaking negatively that we think it is the proper response. When we speak to our coworkers in the office and they ask, "How are you doing?" we say, "I'm here…. Another day, another dollar" or "I just got here and I'm ready to go back home." This kind of negativity has become a way of bonding. Complaining about the job or about the struggles of life has become a way of breaking the ice. You must understand that as you speak these negative thoughts, your ambition – your vision and hope – constantly has to rob from itself in order to compensate. Pretty soon, you have no more positive thoughts or ambition to prompt you to move forward. Your negativity has left you with nothing but a question as to why the final few hours of work seem to last forever.

Your negative talking have sucked dry the last of your energy.

Seeing only the impossibilities produces complaining, which, in essence, is like turning off the lights. You can no longer see your objective, so you just stop. And you are drained not just mentally; imagine the physical energy you will need to push yourself to success? Any successful person knows the importance of energy. You need it to achieve your goals. You need it to perform at your best potential. Successful people do whatever it takes to protect this precious commodity. They eat power bars and other healthy foods, they drink herbal tea, they make sure to get proper rest. Whatever they need to do, they will do to make sure they have the energy to perform at their peak mentally, physically, and spiritually.

To ensure you are not being drained by negative speech, begin reprogramming your spirit and mind to speak positive things every day. Do this during your meditation in the morning or at night. While meditating, begin affirming yourself with the Word of God as it relates to your life and goals. In actuality, what you are doing is watering your seed.

WATERING YOUR SEED

Jesus said, "He that believeth on me, as the scripture hath said, out of his belly shall flow rivers of living water" (John 7:38). How does a farmer cause the seeds he has planted to grow? He waters them. When you speak the Word of God over your field of destiny, you are watering that field and all the seeds you have planted. You must go about realizing your dreams the way a farmer realizes the growth of his crop.

A farmer wakes up early in the morning to attend to a field. Likewise, you must begin your mornings by watering your crops. You must meditate in the morning, affirming yourself with Scripture. Understand that not everyone can wake up at 5:00 a.m. Your morning is whenever you begin your day. Some people's day begins in the evening. Some folks wake up at 7:00 p.m. and work until

6:00 a.m. Their "morning" prayers occur whenever their day begins. The key is to water your seed and receive your daily instructions. You must speak Scriptures such as the following: "The thoughts of the diligent tend only to plenteousness" (Prov. 21:5); "[I have] exceeding great and precious promises" (2 Pet. 1:4); "Blessed shalt [I] be in the city, and blessed shalt [I] be in the field" (Deut. 28:3); "[I am] precious in [God's] sight" (Isa. 43:4); and "All things, whatsoever [I] shall ask in prayer, believing, [I] shall receive" (Matt. 21:22). Begin to daily speak the Word of God over your life and your situations.

It is a given that during your meditation time, the enemy will enter the room and try to convince you that because of your past or because of the mistakes you made the day before, your words are vain. Therefore, it is very important that we understand this next principle:...

Chapter 8
Releasing the Past

"This one thing I do, forgetting those things which are behind, and reaching forth unto those things which are before..." (Phil. 3:13)

P aul realized a certain principle regarding living beyond expectancy that many have yet to discover: releasing the past. This is a critical factor that cannot be overlooked. Whether good or bad, you must release yesterday and embrace today. You must realize that the biggest enemy of today's success is yesterday's success.

Many people hold on to the past for so long that they become crippled by it. They think about how anointed they were, how successful they were, how happy they were – and they refuse to push forward. Their attachment to the past causes them to believe that life cannot improve beyond their point of setback. They can't seem to fathom the idea that even though they fell to the bottom, life isn't over. In fact, it's not that they fell to the bottom at all. When you find yourself in a rut after being on top, don't see yourself as falling; see yourself as transcending the apex of your last level onto the base of your new level.

Let's consider a certain basketball player, for example. In high school, this athlete excelled beyond all of his competitors and teammates. He took his team to the championship, and they won. He scored the most points during the game, retrieved the most rebounds, and made the most assists. After high school, he went to college, and although he made the team, he was benched.

What happened? Was he not a good player after all? Was it that his entire team was inferior? No… the fact is that he had reached a new level at which the players were more skilled and the competitors were bigger and better than he was. So even though he was the best on his high school team, he had to let go of that success and push himself to excel at the new level. It is certainly possible that he will reach a plane of excellence and prominence at this new level. However, he must first realize that he has not fallen to the bottom. He must consider instead that he is realizing the sunset of today's achievement and is moving into the dawn of tomorrow's challenge. Unfortunately, many of us greet a new day with pessimism, or we quit because we can't move beyond our past successes.

When you can see every low point of your life as an opportunity to move to the top, there is nothing that can keep you down. As Christians, we must realize that we have been reborn into victory. There is no such thing as failure. When we are down, we are being moved to another level of anointing. There can be no crown without a cross and no testimony without a test.

RELEASING THE BAD

By the same token, you might find it difficult to let go of the setbacks, pain, and rejection of the past. In fact, you hold tightly to negative influences and traits as sources of comfort. You use them as crutches – a reason to not step out upon your dreams. You convince yourself that since you believe something is impossible, God will exempt you from responsibility. WRONG! Proverbs 22:13 tells us that "the slothful man saith, There is a lion without, I shall be slain in the streets." Here is a man who has heard about a lion that is loose in the area. Now, to the average person, a lion walking around the neighborhood is a pretty good reason to call in for the day. However, this man is considered a sloth and a sluggard, a person who does not want to work and finds ways to get out of his responsibilities.

What does this proverb say to us? It says clearly that there is nothing on earth that should keep you from fulfilling the will of God for your life. When you allow fear of anything (be it failure, sickness, rejection, or even death) to stop you from achieving your purpose, the Bible assesses your reluctance as laziness.

You must release the fears of yesterday's setbacks and move on into today's challenges. Thomas Edison gave the best assessment of past failures (or setbacks). While attempting to create the electric light bulb, Edison failed thousands of times. The leading inventors of the time criticized his work and ostracized him, calling him a madman.

During an interview with a young reporter, Edison was asked, "Why do you continue wasting your time on this foolish experiment after thousands of failed attempts?" Edison responded, "Young man, I have not failed at all. I have successfully pinpointed thousands of ways that will not work, which puts me that much closer to finding the way that will work."

It is only when you can view your past failures as stepping stones to help you grow that you can break the stronghold of fear in your life. If you can evaluate your past experiences and pinpoint where you missed the mark in regard to hearing God, you will be that much closer to finding what you want. Perhaps you missed the mark and now you're afraid to step out into the ministry that God has for you. Just believe that your "failure" was not a failure at all but merely God's way of showing you which way *not* to go.

This results in the "transformation" that Paul speaks of when he writes, "Be not conformed to this world: but be ye transformed by the renewing of your mind" (Rom. 12.2). The mind of Jesus does not hold on to the past. In fact, God Himself says, "I, even I, am he that blotteth out thy transgressions for mine own sake, and will not remember thy sins" (Isa. 43:25). Let's re-emphasize a portion of this scripture. God uses the phrase "for mine own sake." He knows that if He were to continue to look upon the wrong deeds, wickedness, or idolatry of our past, He could never move forward with His plan. Likewise, if you continue to dig up the failures, hurts, pain, and rejection of the past, you will never move forward.

You might wonder how to get past these pains. The answer is simple. We all relive our past in our minds. We might be driving down the street and see a sight that brings back old, painful memories. When these thoughts come, vocally address them; do it immediately – not after dwelling on them – knowing that you are dealing with not mere thoughts but, in fact, a strategic plan of the enemy for maintaining his stronghold on your life. When thoughts of your failures arise, immediately proclaim, "God has delivered me from that failure and I am stronger now through Christ." When thoughts about those who have hurt you arise, say immediately, "I forgive that person for what he/she has done."

Sometimes you will be delivered from certain injuries immediately. But sometimes you will have to fight daily – and sometimes hourly – but the Bible assures us that if we "resist the devil… he will flee" (James 4:7). Once he flees, you must fill your mind with a new word, for the Bible warns us in Matthew 12:43-44 that "when the unclean spirit is gone out of a man, he walketh through dry places, seeking rest, and findeth none. Then he saith, I will return into my house from whence I came out; and when he is come, he findeth it empty, swept, and garnished."

This means that if we don't fill our spirits with the Word of God after He has delivered us from oppression, the negative influence will return, and, as the Word warns us, "the last state of that man [will be] worse than the first" (Matt. 12:43). If you are struggling to forgive someone, begin filling your spirit with the Word of God concerning forgiveness. If you're dealing with past failures and God delivers you from that pain, start filling your spirit with God's Word concerning the victory you possess in Christ. This is how you are to use the Word.

I'm going to stray a bit because many in the Body of Christ don't know how to use the Word of God. There is a catchy acronym using the word "Bible": "Basic Instructions Before Leaving Earth." This is very fitting, particularly in regard to how we should go about using the Word. The Bible is our source of information, but so many of us are more interested in trying to get through the entire Book than ingesting the Word. Many of us are so busy trying to remember numerous passages that we fail to get instructions for life. We find it hard to believe that reading and applying one scripture passage during an entire year would be more acceptable and effective than reading the whole Bible while not applying it. You must find the word for your own life, not concerning yourself with that which is impressive to others. We often take pride in highlighting Scripture, but we refuse to highlight our spirits.

After you have released your past, you are ready to get to work. This is not something you should put off; rather, you should begin to act ...

Chapter 9
Right Now!

I have spoken a great deal about principles that will help you realize your dreams – principles that will help you live beyond expectancy. But there's one more issue that must be addressed. Talking is good, meditating is good, resolving that you are going to change your thinking and step out on the promises of God is good, but there is something more that must be done: you must start working.

If you truly believe that Christ has won the ultimate victory and that you are free to pursue and realize your dreams, then this belief should affect the way you live. When? Right now! You must make up your mind that you are not going to wait until tomorrow or until it's time to go to heaven to get excited about the work of the Lord. You need to get excited right now. You need to step out with a fervent spirit that is willing to lay it all on the line, even when you don't see heaven. Yes, we've heard about the gates of pearl; we've heard about the streets of gold; we've heard about the crystal clear water; we've heard about these and more beautiful features; but we haven't literally seen heaven. Nevertheless, we don't need to wait until we see it to get busy doing what God wants us to do – we need to act right now! Jesus told Thomas, "Blessed are they that have not seen, and yet have believed" (John 20:29). Paul modified the phrase by saying, "We walk by faith, not by sight" (2 Cor. 5:7).

You might ask yourself, "What do faith and belief have to do with works?" We must understand the relationship. The fact is that without faith we truly have no works. "Now wait one minute, Bishop," you might say. "You need to break this down." I will. The equation is really very simple. First of all, we know explicitly from the Word that "without faith it is impossible to please [God]" (Heb. 11:6). Also, we are aware that only those things we do for God will last. Therefore, if God is not pleased with our works, and if the only eternal works are those that we do for God and that meet with His approval, then when we perform works that are not based in faith, they are in vain – useless.

Additionally, we must understand that without works, our faith is dead (see James 2:20). Many sit idly by, gorging themselves with the Word of God and then dragging their full bellies to a nearby couch to sleep it away. I hear God addressing this situation through a proverb: "How long wilt thou sleep, O sluggard? when wilt thou arise out of thy sleep?" (6:9). The Lord despises such waste, as He clearly points out in His parable about the three servants and their talents.

Many who say they believe while refusing to take action are sleeping their way to being taken away: "Every branch in me that beareth not fruit he taketh away…. and cast them into the fire, and they are burned" (John 15:2, 6). This passage shows us clearly that the non-producing Christian is, in a sense, a non-believing Christian. Jesus said it plainly: "He that hath my commandments, and keepeth them, he it is that loveth me.... He that loveth me not keepeth not my sayings" (John 14:21, 24). These commandments to which the Lord makes reference are not merely the Ten Commandments. They include the daily words that God gives – that is, *rhema*. These commandments include the still, small voice that tells us to stop watching TV and pray or that tells us to inform that stranger we just walked past about the goodness of Jesus. These commandments are held in the same esteem as is the *logos* word. One can easily know the *logos* – the revelatory Word – of God, but it takes obedience to God's *rhema* word to incorporate and fully enjoy the *logos*.

VICTORY IN THE NOW

Another reason you must take action right now is because the Word of God tells you there is victory in pushing through; when the devil tries to keep you from doing what you're supposed to do, you have to do it anyhow. The more he wars against you, the more you must persevere because you're dedicated to God's will. You have to stay right where God has positioned you and do what He tells you to do. You must understand that if the devil doesn't want you to do something, then surely something good will come of it, not only for you but also for those around you. Therefore, you need to make up your mind that you are going to do it because the devil doesn't want you to.

Many times, we listen to the devil's seductive reasoning as to why we should be apathetic, why we should sit and do nothing. But the devil doesn't want us to fare well? He wants us to fail, so why would we believe a word he says? From the beginning of time, the devil has sought to destroy the blessings God has given us. He enjoyed some success with Adam and Eve. From the time of the expulsion of Adam and Eve from the Garden to the days of Noah, the devil had a heyday. His plan worked beautifully. Man became so wicked that God couldn't stand even to look at the very creation He so adored.

But something happened. God, in His infinite power, started a new game plan when He whispered in the ear of one of His servants, "Get thee out of thy country, and from thy kindred, and from thy father's house, unto a land that I will shew thee" (Gen. 12:1). I can imagine Satan squinting to hear. "What is God saying to Abram? What's He got under His sleeve? Why is Abram leaving his inheritance and the comfort of his father's home? Oh boy, what is God doing now?"

At that time, God launched His plan, and 42 generations later, that plan came to fruition through the person of Jesus Christ, God's only begotten Son. And when Jesus made His entrance, exit, and reentrance, He conquered and triumphed over all, and now we are part of His Body, which means...

Chapter 10
Christians Never Fail

That's right! Christians do not fail. We have delays, setbacks, frustrations, and potholes, but we don't fail. How can the Body of Christ fail if that very Body has overcome death, hell, and the grave – or when that very Body is seated on the right side of God Himself, who created the heavens and earth, who created the concept of failure and triumph? How can the Body of Christ fail?

As long as there is life in our bodies, we have the opportunity to succeed. Now, it may take some people three months, some three years, some thirty years, and others a lifetime to find success, but there is no failure in God.

When it comes to living beyond expectancy, it is important that you understand this concept because it is the fear of failure that the enemy uses as a foundational deception. Many Christians are afraid to step out because they are afraid to fail. Some are afraid that their inability to perform may cause another to stray. They might misinterpret Proverb 28:10, which warns, "Whoso causeth the righteous to go astray in an evil way, he shall fall himself into his own pit." Like the wicked servant who hid his one talent instead of stepping out in faith and trusting God to bring forth the desired result, some people evaluate their own capabilities as well as limitations and then decide to hide their talents.

It's also important to understand that we as Christians cannot fail because, after all, we are not doing the work. Throughout the Old and New Testaments, God showed His people that He requires only faith and the willingness to obey. He will perform the work. In the Old Testament, God told Joshua, "Every place that the sole of your foot shall tread upon, that have I given unto you" (Josh. 1:3). What was God saying here? He was saying, "Joshua, all I need you to do is step out, and I will take care of the rest." How else do you explain the fortified walls of a city falling down as a result of walking around while screaming at the top of your lungs? God was saying to Joshua, and He is saying to us today, "I just need you to start treading." Many of us have adopted the mindset of defeat and therefore we tread only enough to build a house, to buy a used car, or to obtain a job. But God has given us full rein. We need to tread enough to build a community – an apartment complex; to own several new cars so that we can give some to those who don't have a car; or to own our own business. God has already told us that He has given us all things.

Let's discuss the crux of maximizing your potential—a theme I have lived and preached for over 20 years. A theme that is paramount to living beyond expectancy. God didn't tell Joshua how far to tread. He just promised him that he was guaranteed victory everywhere he trod. God will not force you to start a business. It is up to you to maximize your gifts. The promise God made to you was that when you begin treading upon the land, it has already been won. Victory and prosperity are already assured.

"Only be thou strong and very courageous" (Josh. 1:7). In this verse, we see God telling Joshua, in essence, "When you start treading, don't think the enemy is going to roll out the red carpet for you so that you can obtain your blessings." Many of us fall victim to defeat and despair because we foolishly assume that when God speaks a blessing on us, no opposition will come. But the correct understanding is that, although opposition will indeed come, it will be unable to stop God's blessings. We read scriptures such as Isaiah 54:17 – "No weapon that is formed against thee shall prosper" – and overlook the word "formed." We end up with the flawed interpretation: "No weapon will come against you."

But we need to understand, internalize, and fully prepare for the inevitability of the enemy's attacks against us, our aspirations, and our desires. However, realizing this hard fact does not negate God's command that we start treading. You are dealing with two opposing forces – God's command for you to move forward and the enemy's demand for you to turn back – so what are you going to do? You must be strong and courageous.

Now, let us not misunderstand the command. God is not calling for you to be strong so that, through your prowess, you can bring forth His plan. Zechariah lets us know that it is "not by might, nor by power, but by [God's] spirit" (Zech. 4:6). God is not calling you to be courageous so that, through your own boldness, you can execute His plan. Then why *is* God calling you to be strong and courageous?

STRENGTH

You need strength because the road to your destiny is not an easy one. It's uphill and filled with physical, mental, and spiritual tests and trials. The Christian life, as Langston Hughes' poem *Mother to Son* reads, "ain't… no crystal stair." It's going to have "tacks in it, And splinters,

And boards torn up." You must not be a person who quits or is worn down easily. You can rest assured that your enemy is prepared for a long and drawn-out battle. His goal is to wear you down.

It is commonly known that when Muhammad Ali sparred, he often allowed his partners to attack him without retaliating. He would instruct them to attack his weakest areas. He focused significantly on his body's weakest areas while preparing for his "Rumble in the Jungle" with George Foreman. Foreman was a giant of a boxer with the power of a bull. But Ali, while studying his opponent, realized that along with Foreman's great strength came an excelled rate of energy drainage. Ali realized that if he could strengthen his body to take the blows until all of Foreman's energy was gone, he could defeat the champion – a technique he coined as the "rope-a-dope."

When the fight day came and the battle was on, everyone thought Ali had lost his mind. He just leaned against the ropes, round after round, allowing this giant to bash his body from side to side. Those in his corner were screaming, "Get out of there! Get off of the ropes!" They shouted at the end of every round, "What are you doing? Stick and move!" But all Ali said was, "I know what I'm doing. He's getting tired." Finally, during the 8th round, Foreman's arms began to get heavy. Every muscle he had used to deliver painful blows to Ali's body became weapons against himself. Each punch was more painful to deliver than it was for the opponent to receive. Foreman's blows became slower and his guard became lower until, finally, Ali saw his opportunity and – with a few swift jabs to the face and a powerful uppercut – Foreman was down.

There was no way Ali could have defeated Foreman by going toe-to-toe, but through strengthening the areas that he knew his opponent would attack, Ali was able to endure until the door was open to victory. Likewise, you must strengthen your spirit. You can't fight toe-to-toe with Satan because there is no way you can defeat him in this way. However, by strengthening your spirit via God's Word and obedience to that Word, you will outlast the enemy's attack. Therefore, God calls you to be strong in order to endure the blows of the enemy and keep moving forward. Though God has determined the path to your destiny, He will not prevent opposition from forming because the opposition prepares you for the final destination.

COURAGE

We've all watched the timeless classic *The Wizard of Oz* in which the main character, Dorothy, connects with three companions while traveling the yellow brick road to meet the wizard. The most memorable of these characters is the Cowardly Lion. He stands before Dorothy: the king of jungle, a creature whose strength is unmatched – and yet this lion is a coward, afraid of his own tail. Though he possesses all of the characteristics that symbolize courage, he is a coward at heart.

Courage is the "motor" of strength. With courage, you can take your strength into uncertain terrain and emerge victoriously. Courage catapults strength, converting it into action, which, when empowered by the Holy Spirit, brings about victory.

Just ask David. In Saul's army were the finest of soldiers. The Bible reveals that Saul hand-picked his soldiers: "Saul chose him three thousand men of Israel" (1 Sam. 13:2).

So it seems strange that when Goliath called for the greatest among the Hebrew troops to present themselves in battle, no one in the camp was itching to represent the army. Despite all their strength and skill, the men had no courage.

On the flipside, there was "ruddy... beautiful" David (1 Sam. 16:12). If we study his life, we find that he was endowed with a great deal of strength (including strength of faith and character) and skill of weaponry, particularly the sling. However, strength did not catapult David into battle with Goliath. Every man in the Hebrew army had strength, but only David had the motor of courage to drive him into action. I particularly appreciate the wording of the New King James version of the Bible, which reads, "David hurried and ran toward the army to meet the Philistine" (1 Sam. 17:48). David's decision to make haste to the battle indicated his courage.

David hurried into battle because he did not want to give place to doubt or second-guessing. Many times God will tell us to step out in faith and perform a certain work, but we procrastinate. The more time we spend thinking about it, the more we begin to doubt the voice of God. David knew that if he sat down and thought about what he was about to do – what God was sending him to do – he would begin to focus on the difference in size between himself and Goliath. He would begin to hear Saul's doubt-filled words in his head: "Thou art not able to go against this Philistine to fight with him: for thou art but a youth, and he a man of war from his youth" (1 Sam. 17:33).

Living Beyond Expectancy

David decided that he was going to allow his motor of courage to catapult him into doing God's will. Now, what was the difference between David and the thousands of other soldiers? Physically, the others were greater than David. Intellectually speaking, there must have been older and wiser soldiers at hand. So all of them had strength of some sort. Likewise, we all have strength, but many of us lack the motor of courage – for courage is not an absence of fear in the midst of adversity but a willingness to move forward despite that fear. By refusing to be courageous – because, in fact, being courageous is a choice – we don't utilize the strength that God has given us.

I am reminded of a parable by Mark Twain entitled *The Greatest General*:

A man died and met Saint Peter at the gates of heaven. Recognizing the saint's knowledge and wisdom, the man asked a question: "Saint Peter, I have been interested in military history for many years. Tell me, who was the greatest general of all time?"

Peter quickly responded, "Oh, that is a simple question. The greatest general is right over there."

The man looked where Peter was pointing and said, "You must be mistaken. I knew that man on earth, and he was just a common laborer."

"That's right," Peter remarked, "But had he been a general, he would have been the greatest general of all time."

No doubt the laborer lacked the courage to step into what obviously was a calling to the armed services. He would have been the greatest general. God had placed in him the strength to lead people to victory. God had given him strength of strategy and implementation. Instead, he had allowed fear to keep him from moving forward in his strength – in his calling. This man did not just fear war, he feared leadership, for he worked as a mere laborer. He didn't even have the courage to step forward in the job market. The very thing he feared – being a leader – was the very purpose of his existence.

Living Beyond Expectancy

The enemy knows his job. He knows that the only way to stop someone from moving forward in his or her destiny is to make him or her fear it beforehand. (Now, pull out your highlighter). The very door through which you are afraid to walk may well be the door to your purpose.

The Word states that "God hath not given us the spirit of fear" (2 Tim. 1:7), so the feeling of fear – that is, a debilitating compulsion that causes one to avoid or flee a person, place or situation – is of the enemy. Fear must be confronted head-on. Joyce Meyer is best known for saying, "Do it afraid." You must step out and be courageous in spite of fear. Only then can you utilize the strength God has given you and get into position for God to work.

Once you realize that you can never fail, you can step out and begin treading the land with strength and courage – and above all, stay...

Chapter 11
Positive in Spite of Discouragement

Earlier, I made reference to David's conversation with King Saul. David, completely convinced he could fight Goliath and win, told the king the good news: "Don't worry about this giant. I'll take him out." But all Saul could see was the negative – the apparent facts. "You can't fight him," he said. "You're just a boy and he's a champion warrior. He's forgotten more about killing than you've learned during your whole life."

Many times, we step out with earnest optimism to do God's will and then make the mistake of sharing our aspirations with anyone and everyone. What we get in return is a trough full of negative reasoning, evil foreboding, and doubt-filled questioning. We've got to resolve to never allow anyone to keep us from doing what God wants us to do. We have to come to the point where we tell the world, "It's my time to step out on the strength of

God. It's my time to do what seems impossible and to receive the blessings of God! I'm not asking you to believe it, I'm not asking you whether or not you want it to happen, and I'm not asking you about your feelings. No matter what you think, I'm going to realize my dreams."

Do not let discouragement over apparent lack of results keep you from working. You might start something and expect to see immediate and positive changes, but many times it doesn't happen like that. Thomas Edison commented, "Failure is really a matter of conceit. People don't want to work hard because, in their conceit, they imagine they'll succeed without ever making an effort."

You might say, "I thought I would see results by now." But just continue to work. If results don't happen tomorrow, just keep working. After thirty days, if nothing happens, don't worry about it — just keep going. If a year passes, just keep working.

A certain mother in my church had been dealing with high blood pressure and other health abnormalities for 28 years, but because she never stopped trusting God for her healing she is healed today. Let me tell you what the devil won't tell you. You should not be bothered if your blessing does not manifest when you think it should. Why shouldn't that bother you? Because as long as you are working toward your promise, you are in a positive position, and as long as you remain positive, you are guaranteed to see positive results eventually. As Proverb 14:23 promises, "In all labour there is profit [an advantageous gain or return]."

What the devil wants to do is cause you to become discouraged during that first hour of anticipation. Once he plants a string of negative thoughts into your spirit, you will start walking in that negativity, and as long as you walk in negativity you'll get negative results, for "as [a person] thinketh in his [or her] heart, so is he [or she]," according to Proverb 23:7. So what you need to do is stay positive in spite of discouragement because if you do so you'll have positive results.

Living Beyond Expectancy

Imagine you need a thousand dollars. A positive move is to save $10 at a time; as long as you can save $10, you're "in the positive." Eventually, if you save $10 a week for long enough, you'll have your thousand dollars. But if you allow negative thoughts in and don't save anything, you're not going to have anything in the end. You need to understand that when you allow yourself to complain and think negatively, the only outcome is disappointment and failure. That's that.

Everything you do produces a result. Why choose to allow a negative result? What harm will it do to continue to think and speak positively about your situations, desires, and/or dreams? If nothing else, at least you'll sleep well at night.

A positive outlook will render positive results even if those results are not what you expected. Even if you don't reach your goals, you will achieve something of worth. The adage says, "Reach for the moon because, even if you don't make it, you'll be among the stars." God wants you to allow nothing less than positive thoughts into your spirit. He wants you to release the desire for immediate gratification. As John C. Maxwell states in his book, *Your Attitude: Key to Success*, "Success is achieved in inches, not in miles." Your mindset needs to be, "I'm going to get there, even if it is one step at a time! I started at the same time as did the others, and they've already made it. I praise God with them and appreciate what's happening in their lives, and even though I didn't make it as quickly as they did, I'm still going to make it. I know I'm going to get there because I'm not going to give up; I'm not going to become discouraged; their success will not hinder me. I praise God for where they are, but I'm on my way too."

You must never give up on the call of God on your life, knowing that your work has…

Chapter 12
Eternal Value

I will conclude this book with an admonition: let us begin moving in the purpose God has for us, knowing that there's more at stake than a mere few dollars; there's more at stake than our vapor of life. There's eternal value in our work.

When you come to the realization that your work has eternal value, you will also realize the urgency of God's calling on your life. You don't have time for lollygagging. Jesus said it best: "I must work the works of him that sent me, while it is day: the night cometh, when no man can work" (John 9:4). There is soon coming the conclusion to all things, and when it comes will you be like the wicked servant who did nothing, or will you be like the faithful servant who took his talents and doubled them? I don't want to have an negative balance when God calls me home.

Bishop Jerry L. Maynard

Have you ever made a decision that was good for the moment but detrimental in the long run? The work you are doing for God is not just for the present — it has eternal significance. You have to be dedicated not just for what you might gain today; you must also look ahead to what's going to happen tomorrow. The Word of God makes a strong point concerning this very issue in 1 Kings 17.

A widow woman was on her way to make a last little bit of bread for herself and her son before they died as a result of famine. Instead she blessed the prophet Elijah with that bread and relied on God to bless her with more.

Now, the Lord could have blessed her with a one-time fill-up and that would have lasted that day or perhaps a few weeks. But that's not what He did because He didn't want to limit her blessing to the present; He wanted to provide an eternal blessing. So He blessed her by not merely filling the barrel but replenishing it daily so that every time she went to the barrel she was able to retrieve enough meal to feed herself, her son, and the prophet. God was concerned about the woman's tomorrow.

There's more to God's tomorrow than meets the eye. God was concerned about the widow's physical tomorrow; this is clear. He wanted to ensure she had food for her physical body. But also consider that if it had been noised abroad that the woman had an overflowing, self-refilling barrel of meal, she would probably have been in danger. Thieves, robbers, and desperately hungry people in general would not have hesitated to take what she had by any means necessary. Likewise, you might wonder why the sky has not opened up and poured down your blessings. You might wonder why your blessings seem to come in sprinkles. Though it seems difficult to believe, God is protecting you from the thieves, robbers, and desperate clingers who might destroy you if they were to find out what God had tucked away for you. God knows the perfect time for your increase. He knows whether certain "friends" that you trust would turn out to be detractors or whether certain neighbors would turn out to be thieves and robbers.

God also was concerned about the widow's spiritual tomorrow. When you first read this story, did you wonder why God didn't fill the barrel completely? Why did He fill it just enough for that day? Understand that God's main objective in all His dealings with humanity is to bring about reconciliation. More so than just providing food for the widow and the prophet, God wanted to develop in them a trust and dependence upon Himself.

God did not fill the barrel completely because, if He had, the woman would have taken her blessings for granted.

Many times, when things are going well for us, we forget about God. We stop praying, start missing church services, and begin enjoying the gifts more than the Giver. This is not because we don't love God but because we feel we don't have need of anything, so we don't call on Him.

Living Beyond Expectancy

When we have a good-paying job, we have no reason to seek God's instruction so that we might enjoy another meal. When our health is good, we forget to show God appreciation for waking us up and starting us on our way without pain. It is only during those tight, painful moments that many of us recognize God's presence.

God knows this, and therefore we often receive our blessing little by little. God knows that if we were to get it all at once, our spiritual tomorrow would be harmed if not destroyed. God is not interested in merely supplying your need. He is even more concerned with developing you. He brings about constructive development through your moments of lack. This is why He hates complaining, which is a slap in His face.

God is trying to develop us into kings, queens, princes and priests, but because the training is uncomfortable we complain against Him.

Imagine loving a child so much that you decide one day to take him/her to Disney World for the first time.

However, because the journey to Disney World takes a long time, the child begins to complain that you never do anything nice for him. All of his friends have already been to Disney World so evidently you do not care about him. You explain, "Listen, it takes a little while to get to Disney World, but when we get there it will be more wonderful than you can imagine."

Even so, though the child knows he is en route to Disney World, he talks only about how unhappy he is and how you do nice things for everyone but him. After a while, you're going to turn the car around and tell him that the trip is off and the only place he is going is home and to bed.

It sounds almost ridiculous that a child would do this, yet we do it to God all the time. When we don't see immediate, *big* results, we start to complain. Even as God is trying to develop us by taking us through the process of maturation so that our works will last and not be burned by the fires of proving, we complain. While we seem to think there will be no reward; we don't realize that God is bringing about eternal value from our efforts.

Jesus utilized the farmer in many parables because the life of a farmer best reflects that of a Christian. We are laborers who spend time sowing seed, watering, and waiting. We cannot grow weary in the waiting because it is during this time of waiting that God is doing His work.

After we give, we need to wait patiently, knowing that the soil of God's grace is fertilizing our seeds of faith and will bring about an eternal harvest. This is the reason He wants you to be dedicated. He wants to know that if He tells you that you are healed, you won't give up when you feel pain. When He tells you that He's going to bless you with a house even though you're about to be evicted from an apartment, you won't give up. When He tells you that if you pay your tithe He will "open you the windows of heaven, and pour you out a blessing, that there shall not be room enough to receive it" (Mal 3:10), you won't give up when it seems you have less money now than you did before. He needs to know that you won't give up when He tells you that your marriage will improve but it seems it's getting worse.

God wants you to be dedicated and determined! What does He want you to be dedicated to and determined about? His Word. He said it all in His Word; and since His word said it, you can't look at results. You must look only at His Word. You can't look at conditions; you must look at His Word. You can't act according to what you see; you must act according to what He said. You can't always live according to what is shown, but by what is known.

You must know that despite the waiting, the pain, the sacrifice and heartache, your labor has so much more significance than the moment. You are not a character in some majestic video game who provides a moment of jollity for God. You are a thread in the fabric of humanity and your very existence impacts the whole of humanity.

Living Beyond Expectancy

Had Joseph's brothers not sold him into slavery, he would have never become the next highest leader of Egypt, thereby allowing him to save the tribe of Jacob, which lead to the birth of Jesus, which lead to the salvation of all humanity—including you and me. Our lives have eternal value.

Conclusion

Throughout this book I have done my best to explain a sure way to living a life that exceeds your expectations and the expectations of this world. The Body of Christ is a victorious one, and the world should see within us the reason we serve God. If the Body looks weak and unimpressive, why would anyone on the outside choose to be a part of it? This book makes it clear that true life cannot be attained through carnal means.

Many times, when we read books such as this one, we begin thinking about driving a nice car, wearing impressive clothes, and living in the best of homes. However, this is a carnal idea. The true, foundational message of this book concerns spiritual prosperity. Matthew 6:33 encourages us, "Seek ye first the kingdom of God, and his righteousness; and all these things shall be added unto you." God wants us to have the best the world has to offer, but it can only be realized through the Spirit.

Living Beyond Expectancy

It is my prayer, as it was the Apostle John's, that the readers of this book prosper even as his or her soul prospers (see 3 John 1:2). Living beyond expectancy is a spiritual phenomenon. It involves material goods just as much as it involves health, peace, and joy. As well, it embraces abundance of finances, friends, and family. By following the steps presented in this book – living in the spirit, walking in spiritual wisdom, properly preparing for your purpose, knowing your position in Christ, understanding the virtues of the tongue, releasing the past, getting busy on your purpose right now, knowing that you cannot fail, staying positive in spite of discouragement, and seeking the eternal value of your work, you can expect to see results beyond your expectations.

Living Beyond Expectancy

Bishop Jerry L. Maynard

For more information about Bishop Maynard and his ministry, to order more books, or to contact J.L. Maynard Ministries, visit

www.BishopMaynard.com

More About Bishop Jerry L. Maynard

Bishop Maynard completed graduate and postgraduate studies in Psychology and Social Sciences at Indiana University and the Doctorates Division of Cross Roads Bible College. Bishop Maynard, a native of Indiana, served as Director of the Muncie Indiana Human Rights Commission from 1967-1970, a member of the Indiana and United States Civil Rights Commission from 1970-1981, and the President's Domestic Policy Committee from 1977-1983. He is the recipient of the highest civilian award of the state of Indiana, "Sagamore of the Wabash."

A noted speaker, Bishop Maynard has lectured at Ball State University, Taylor University, Indiana and Indiana State Universities, Cross Roads Bible College, Clark University and keynoted the nationally know "Soul Winners" Conference.

Bishop Maynard's concern for the growth and edification of God's people extends beyond the church. In 1997, as Cathedral Of Praise (formerly Pentecostal Tabernacle) began planning for the construction of the new 1800 seat Sanctuary and Worship Center, Bishop Maynard chose Church Builders United, a partnership of minority-owned contractors. In addition, minority and women-owned businesses worked as sub-contractors on the project.

Bishop Maynard further insisted that the labor force be made up of a significant number of minorities. Thus, approximately eighty-percent of the laborers working on the construction of the facility were African-American and Latino. Other churches building new facilities are now patterning this model. For his efforts, and his many contributions for the establishment of entrepreneurial enterprises, Bishop Maynard received the "R. H. Boyd Business Advocate of the Year 1999" award.

Bishop Maynard, a pioneer in ministry, utilizes new technology and the media to reach the masses. The Cathedral of Praise daily radio broadcasts, weekly telecast on Cable/TV, and website are ways in which Bishop Maynard delivers his messages of "Maximizing Your Potential."

Bishop Maynard is married to Dr. Mary T. Maynard who is retired from serving as Deputy Superintendent of Schools in DeKalb County Georgia.

www.TrueVinePublishing.org

www.ingramcontent.com/pod-product-compliance
Lightning Source LLC
Chambersburg PA
CBHW031422290426
44110CB00011B/485